Contents

For attention of the learner

You are not allowed to copy any information from this book and use it as your own evidence. That would count as plagiarism, which is taken very seriously and may result in disqualification. If you are in any doubt at all please speak to your teacher.

Introduction

Introducing Retail Business is an internally assessed optional unit with two learning aims. It focuses on the way in which retailing has developed, the types of businesses that operate in the sector and the job roles that are available. The unit provides an opportunity to explore the links between retailing and the external environment.

This book includes:

- Guidance on each learning aim – all the topics in the learning aims should be studied, and the book includes useful suggestions for each. Examples are included, but these could be replaced by local examples from your area.
- Evidence generated by a learner for each assessment criterion with feedback from an assessor. The assessor has highlighted where the evidence is sufficient to satisfy the grading criterion and provided developmental feedback when additional work is required. This material provides support for assessment.
- Examples of assignment briefs with clear guidance on the evidence you will need to generate and submit for each grading criterion, and the format in which the evidence should be submitted.

Answers to the knowledge recap questions provided in the learning aim summaries can be found at the back of the guide.

Command words

You will find the following command words in the assessment criteria for each unit. These descriptions may help you to understand what you have to submit for each Pass, Merit and Distinction grading criterion.

- **Outline** – write a clear description but not a detailed one.
- **Explain** – set out in detail the meaning of something, with reasons. More difficult than 'describe' or 'list' so it can help to give an example to show what you mean. Start by introducing the topic then give the 'how' or 'why'.
- **Compare** – identify the main factors that apply in two or more situations and explain the similarities and differences or advantages and disadvantages.
- **Assess** – give careful consideration to all the factors or events that apply and identify which are the most important or relevant.
- **Describe** – give a clear description that includes all the relevant features – think of it as 'painting a picture with words'.
- **Justify** – give reasons or evidence to support your opinion or view to show how you arrived at your conclusions.

Learning aim A
Explore the structure and organisation of retail business

Learning aim A looks at the structure of the retail sector and the types of businesses that operate within the sector. It also looks at job roles and progression routes within the sector.

Assessment criteria

2A.P1 Describe the sub-sector, channels, format, size, ownership and location of two retail businesses operating in different sub-sectors.

2A.P2 Describe the functions of two job roles in store operations and their progression routes.

2A.P3 Explain, using examples, the role of two businesses that support retail businesses.

2A.P4 Describe how two retail businesses operating in different sub-sectors make use of non-outlet retailing.

2A.P5 Describe the aims and objectives of two retail businesses operating in different sub-sectors.

2A.M1 Assess two different types of ownership of selected retail businesses.

2A.M2 Explain how and why two retail businesses operating in different sub-sectors use aims and objectives.

2A.D1 Evaluate how two retail businesses operating in different sub-sectors measure their performance, with reference to key performance indicators (KPIs).

The nature of retailing

What is retailing?

Studied ☐

Retail is the sale of goods or services from a business to a customer. The retailer will purchase goods in large quantities directly from large manufacturers or from wholesalers and then sell the goods in smaller quantities to its customers. The retailer needs to price the products so that they cover the cost of buying the goods from the wholesaler or manufacturer and any advertising, while making a profit.

The relationship between wholesaling and manufacturing

The manufacturer is responsible for turning raw materials into useful products. When the products have been produced the manufacturer will sell them to a wholesaler. The wholesaler will buy in large quantities from the manufacturer and then store the products until they are required by a retailer.

Wholesalers are often referred to as 'middle men' because they sit between the manufacturer and the retailer. Lots of people feel that if the manufacturer sold directly to the retailer this could reduce the price paid by both the retailer and the customer.

The supply chain

The supply chain consists of all the elements involved: from the customer wanting a product and the manufacturer making the product, to the customer receiving the product. The supply chain therefore includes all of the processes and businesses involved in getting the product made and placed in the hands of the customer. The elements involved in the supply chain will include suppliers, manufacturers, transport, warehouses and storage, and retailers. For the supply chain to be efficient all businesses need to be motivated and committed.

Retail channels

Retail channels are the different routes available for a retailer to get its products and services to its target market. The retailer needs to find the most appropriate way in which to sell its products and this could be:

- a **shop or store** – on a housing estate, in a town or city centre, or at an outlet centre
- a **showroom** – which provides the opportunity to display the products
- **e-tailing** – short for electronic retailing, where products are sold on the internet
- **mobile technology** – provides the opportunity to sell or buy from home, the office or while travelling
- **catalogues** – these can be delivered to all homes in a selected area or to existing customers; the customer can place an order by post, telephone or through an agent

BTEC
BUSINESS
ASSESSMENT GUIDE

Level 2

Uni

HODDER
EDUCATION
AN HACHETTE UK COMPANY

The sample learner answers provided in this assessment guide are intended to give guidance on how a learner might approach generating evidence for each assessment criterion. Answers do not necessarily include all of the evidence required to meet each assessment criterion. Assessor comments intend to highlight how sample answers might be improved to help learners meet the requirements of the grading criterion but are provided as a guide only. Sample answers and assessor guidance have not been verified by Edexcel and any information provided in this guide should not replace your own internal verification process.

Any work submitted as evidence for assessment for this unit must be the learner's own. Submitting as evidence, in whole or in part, any material taken from this guide will be regarded as plagiarism. Hodder Education accepts no responsibility for learners plagiarising work from this guide that does or does not meet the assessment criteria.

The sample assignment briefs are provided as a guide to how you might assess the evidence required for all or part of the internal assessment of this Unit. They have not been verified or endorsed by Edexcel and should be internally verified through your own Lead Internal Verifier as with any other assignment briefs, and/or checked through the BTEC assignment checking service.

The authors and publishers would like to thank the following for the use of photographs in this volume:

Figure 1.1 © Pavel Losevsky – Fotolia; figure 1.2 © Imagestate Media (John Foxx); Figure 1.3 © Monkey Business – Fotolia; Figure 1.4 © dell – Fotolia; Figure 2.1 © Aleš Nowák – Fotolia; Figure 2.2 © Sean Gladwell – Fotolia

Every effort has been made to trace and acknowledge ownership of copyright. The publishers will be glad to make suitable arrangements with any copyright holders whom it has not been possible to contact.

Orders: please contact Bookpoint Ltd, 130 Milton Park, Abingdon, Oxon OX14 4SB. Telephone: (44) 01235 827720. Fax: (44) 01235 400454. Lines are open from 9 a.m. to 5 p.m., Monday to Saturday, with a 24-hour message answering service. You can also order through our website www.hoddereducation.co.uk

If you have any comments to make about this, or any of our other titles, please send them to educationenquiries@hodder.co.uk

British Library Cataloguing in Publication Data

A catalogue record for this title is available from the British Library

ISBN: 978 1444 18689 5

This edition published 2013

Impression number   10 9 8 7 6 5 4 3 2 1

Year   2016, 2015, 2014, 2013

Copyright © 2013 Ian Gunn

Cover photo from © Elnur – Fotolia

Typeset by Integra Software Services Pvt. Ltd., Pondicherry, India.

Printed in Dubai for Hodder Education,
An Hachette UK Company,
338 Euston Road,
London NW1 3BH by

- **home shopping** – customers can buy from catalogues, television adverts or the internet in the comfort of their own home
- **market stalls** – these may be permanent indoor stalls in a town centre or stalls on a weekly outdoor site that move from location to location.

Retail sub-sectors

The retail sector is divided into several product-related subdivisions including:

- **Automotive** – for example spare parts for cars or bikes, tools and oil.
- **Clothing** – for example trousers, dresses, jumpers, coats and underwear.
- **Electrical goods** – for example kettles, microwaves and televisions.
- **Food and groceries** – for example milk, bread, cheese and eggs.
- **Footwear** – for example shoes, boots and slippers.
- **DIY** – for example paint, wallpaper, wood, nails and tools.
- **Homewares** – for example chairs, tables and beds.
- **Music and video** – for example DVDs, videos and games.
- **Specialised stores** – for example pet stores, books, and items for hobbies such as golf and camping.
- **Personal care** – for example products for the skin and hair.
- **Second-hand goods** – for example charity shops and second-hand stores.

Figure 1.1 Clothing is a sub-sector of the retail industry

Knowledge recap questions

1. Why is it better for a manufacturer to sell to a wholesaler rather than directly to a retailer?

2. State the supply chain involved in getting frozen peas on to the shelves of a retailer.

3. What is meant by the term 'retail sub-sector'?

4. List four examples of sub-sectors other than DIY.

Retail business ownership

Businesses that operate in the retail sector vary in size, from a small sole trader, which is run predominately by the owner, to a large public limited company, which is run by an elected board of directors.

Sole traders

Studied ☐

A sole trader is when just one person sets up the business. It is the easiest type of business to set up.

There are several **advantages** of being a sole trader. The decisions are made by the owner and the owner will keep all the profits. There is very little administration required in setting up the business.

The main **disadvantages** are that the owner is responsible if the business fails and for any claims from customers for accidents or faulty goods. If the owner is ill there may be no one to take over; the owner may have limited skills. After the initial start many sole traders cannot expand because they may have limited money (capital) of their own to keep putting in and may not want to take out a loan. This may limit what the sole trader can do even if demand for their products is there.

Partnerships

Studied ☐

A partnership is an agreement between two or more people to set up a business venture and is relatively easy to set up.

The **advantages** of a partnership are that, because there is more than one person, it is easier to raise finance. The partners will be able to support one another and may have different skills and attributes that they can bring to the business. There will always be someone to discuss ideas with and partners to share the workload.

The **disadvantages** are that the profits will have to be shared, and each partner is liable for any bad decisions or any loss incurred. The main disadvantage of a partnership is unlimited liability, which means that each partner is liable for any debts. It may also take longer to make a decision because you have to consult the other partners and you may not always agree.

Private limited companies

Studied ☐

A private limited company is usually medium to large in size and the shareholders (who are often the directors too) want to keep their business separate from their personal interests and risks, so that if the business goes bust they only lose what they invest. They can only get money from private investors, usually people they know.

The main **advantage** is limited liability, but other advantages are that it is easy to raise finance and the business is likely to have employees with more skills and attributes.

The main **disadvantages** are that profits are shared and that decision making may take longer because more employees will be involved. The slow decision making may make it slower to respond to changes in the market.

Public limited companies

Studied ☐

A public limited company (PLC) is a large business that sells its shares on the stock market and is owned by its shareholders. The main difference from a private limited company is that the general public can buy shares in a PLC.

The main **advantage** is that the business can raise money more easily and that it can employ people with specialist skills and knowledge.

The **disadvantages** are that the profits are divided between the shareholders and that decisions are made by an elected board of directors.

Franchises

Studied ☐

A franchise is when an owner of a successful business (known as a franchisor) gives permission to another person or business (known as a franchisee) to open up a business using their ideas, products and business name. The franchisee will pay a fee and a percentage of their sales revenue to the franchisor. The franchisee will own the retail shop but the franchisor will keep control over how the products are sold and marketed.

The main **advantages** are that the business idea and brand name are already a success (for example, McDonald's or Subway). The new franchisee will be provided with training and support.

The main **disadvantages** are that there may be restrictions on what can be done, and set up costs may be expensive. A percentage of the profits will go to the franchisor.

Knowledge recap questions

1. What is the main difference between a private limited company and a public limited company?

2. What is the difference between a franchisor and a franchisee?

3. Why would two friends interested in setting up a hairdressing business go into partnership rather than have two separate businesses?

Learning aim A: Explore the structure and organisation of retail business

5

Retail outlets

There is a wide choice of retail outlets, from a small micro-shop that specialises in one type of product, to a large hypermarket where you can buy just about anything.

- A **micro business** is often a small sole trader and occasionally a partnership which has up to nine staff. A micro business has often been developed from a hobby or interest.
- **Small- and medium-sized enterprises (SMEs)** are businesses that employ fewer than 250 staff.
- **Large outlets** can be discount designer outlets or factory outlets. A discount designer outlet can be several stores situated in one area that sell a wide range of products from clothes to household items. The attraction for shoppers is that products from well-known brands are stated to be cheaper than those sold in high-street stores.

A retail outlet could also be:

- An **independent trader** – retail outlets that are individually owned and managed, and do not form part of a chain of shops. The independent trader will make the decisions and so is responsible for the success or failure of the business.
- A **convenience store** – a small local shop that opens long hours and sells a small range of grocery and other household products. Prices in convenience stores are usually a little higher than those in supermarkets.
- **Symbol groups** – suppliers to independent stores or small supermarkets. They do not have their own stores but have become popular by selling their services to existing stores. Spar is one of the more recognised symbol groups.
- A **specialist outlet** – an outlet that sells products for one target market. Examples of specialisms are books, camera equipment, or items for camping and clothing for outdoor activities.
- A **market stall** – sells a range of different products. In some towns there are permanent sites for markets that are open six or seven days a week. In other towns a market visits once or twice a week. At Christmas time there are often special markets that sell products from different countries.
- A **kiosk** – a small retail store. Kiosks are often located at rail or bus stations and sometimes in town centres. They mainly sell newspapers, cigarettes, sweets and drinks.
- A **multiple/chain store** – stores that belong to the same owners and which sell the same products but in different areas of the country. Most of the stores will have the same layout and all displays and posters will be in same format. All stores in the chain will have the same discounts and special offers. Chain

stores can be found in most town or city centres and on retail parks. An example of a chain store is BHS.

- A **discount store** – sells products at a price lower than those in other retail outlets. Most discount stores sell a wide range of products, from food to garden furniture, but others may focus on one specific range such as clothing. A lot of discount stores do sell brand-name products but at a cheaper price than convenience stores and some supermarkets. There is usually a discount store in most town or city centres.
- A **co-operative** – these sell a variety of products. The stores that belong to the co-operative will work together to reduce the costs of purchasing and marketing their products.
- **Franchising** – selling products under the brand and trademark of the franchisor. The franchisee will own the outlet but will only sell the franchisor's products. Examples of franchises are McDonald's and Domino's Pizza. Franchised outlets are located in most town or city centres and on most retail parks.
- A **superstore** – a large retail outlet that sells a wide variety of products from groceries and clothes to household items. Some superstores may focus on one type of product, such as electrical items or household furniture. Superstores are usually located on the outskirts of a town or city.
- A **hypermarket** – a very large retail outlet. Hypermarkets are usually a mix of a supermarket and a department store and sell a very wide range of products, from groceries to DIY products. Hypermarkets are usually located on the outskirts of towns or cities.
- A **department store** – sells a wide range of products that are divided into departments; such as toys, ladies clothing and menswear. Department stores are located in most town and city centres.

Knowledge recap questions

1. Define each of the following by the number of people it employs:

    a. Micro business

    b. SME

    c. Large outlet.

2. How does a department store like Selfridges differ from a chain store like Marks & Spencer?

3. Why would customers still shop at a local convenience store even though the prices are higher than at a supermarket?

Non-outlet retailing

Customers today may work long unsociable hours or have young families and do not have time to visit the town centre or a retail outlet. These customers will look for a more convenient way to shop for the things they need. There are several types of non-outlet retailing.

Mail order

Studied ☐

Mail order is where the customer can place an order by mail or telephone. The product range is vast, from clothes to household furniture. When the order is placed the items will be delivered to the customer.

E-tailing

Studied ☐

E-tailing is buying goods on the internet. The internet allows the customer to shop 24 hours a day, seven days a week, and they can buy just about anything. The customer can search the internet for the item they want and then place an order. It is quick and easy to compare prices, but customers may have to pay for postage.

Catalogues

Studied ☐

Catalogues provide a wide choice for customers. The customer can make their choice from clothing to household furniture in the comfort of their home. When the order has been placed by telephone or mail the products are delivered to the customer's home.

Telephone selling

Studied ☐

Telephone selling is when a business contacts customers by phone to try and sell their products. A business may use telephone selling to contact existing customers to inform them about new or existing products or may just cold-call customers to try to generate sales. Double glazing and insurance companies are examples of business that use telephone selling.

Vending machines

Studied ☐

Vending machines generally hold only one type of product, such as chocolate bars, but will offer a choice of different brands. Other products sold in vending machines include crisps, cold drinks and hot beverages. The vending machine will release the selected product after the customer has inserted sufficient money to pay for the item. Vending machines can be found in many different locations including bus or rail stations, cinemas and leisure centres.

Shopping channels

Studied ▢

Shopping channels are television channels that advertise and demonstrate a wide range of products, such as jewellery, skin products and kitchen appliances. The orders are placed by phone and the products are delivered to the door.

Location

Choosing the right location can be the difference between a successful business and one that fails. A retail business will need to consider the cost of transporting products from suppliers to the store, ease of access for their target market, access to sufficient employees with the correct qualifications and skills, competition and the availability of any government assistance for locating in an area.

A retail business can choose to locate in a range of locations.

City and town centres

Studied ▢

A business will need to find a location in the town or city that will provide access to their target market. The price to purchase or rent a retail outlet in a town or city may be high; parking could be limited and may be free or very expensive. The business will have the opportunity to attract customers who work in the town, but there may also be more competition.

Out of town

Studied ▢

Lots of large supermarkets and specialist stores have chosen to move away from city- and town-centre locations to cheaper locations on the outskirts of cities or towns. The majority of out-of-town stores provide longer opening hours and free parking for customers, and most will have a cafe and toilet facilities. The rise in petrol prices may have an impact on customers using out-of-town stores.

Figure 1.2 Out-of-town stores provide facilities such as free parking

District

Studied ▢

Retail stores will choose a location where they can attract customers and some may choose to locate close to residential areas or in locations close to other businesses. The retail outlet will need to decide if it wants to locate close to competitors, where customers can compare prices.

Retail parks

Studied ☐

Customers can find a choice of different retail stores in one place at a retail park. Most retail parks provide free parking. Customers are able to compare prices and quality from store to store.

Primary locations

Studied ☐

Primary locations may be more convenient for customers but are more expensive to rent or buy. A primary location may be easy to access for employees but may also be located close to competitors.

Secondary locations

Studied ☐

Secondary locations may be cheaper to rent or buy, have less competition and usually have free parking for customers.

Knowledge recap questions

1. Why would a business selling vacuum cleaners use a shopping channel rather than just a catalogue?

2. State one advantage and one disadvantage of buying a prom dress on the internet.

3. How does mail-order selling work?

4. Why would electrical retailer like Currys prefer to open an outlet on a retail park than in a town centre?

5. Businesses of a similar type, such as car showrooms, are often located close together. Why do they choose this method of retailing?

6. State two features of:
   a. Primary locations
   b. Secondary locations.

Jobs in retail business

There are several different job roles and progression routes available in the retail sector.

- A **cashier** is responsible for taking payment for products. They need to know how to take payment by cash, debit or credit card. They may also be responsible for scanning products and helping customers to pack their bags.
- A **customer service employee** is responsible for providing customers with information and advice, and for dealing with customer problems and complaints. Good customer service helps to build trust and loyalty; poor customer service may result in customers shopping elsewhere.

Figure 1.3 A good customer service employee should be able to advise customers on the products available

- The role of a **retail assistant** will depend on the size of the retail outlet. They could be responsible for scanning products and taking payments, restocking shelves, providing information and advice, and dealing with customer problems and complaints. In smaller retail outlets a retail assistant could also be responsible for stocktaking and reordering.
- A **sales-floor assistant** is responsible for providing customers with advice and guidance when selecting their products and making sure that the shelves are fully stocked. They will also be responsible for ensuring the shop is neat and tidy, and that any hazards such as wet floors are dealt with.

- A **sales-floor supervisor** is responsible for managing the staff on the sales floor. They will make sure that all customers are provided with sufficient and efficient help in choosing their products and making purchases. In a large retail outlet the sales-floor supervisor may also be responsible for producing staff rotas and staff training.

- A **stockroom assistant** is responsible for unpacking deliveries and moving the stock to the storeroom or sales floor. They will also be responsible for keeping the stockroom or warehouse clean and tidy. In a small retail outlet the stockroom assistant may be responsible for checking that products are not damaged and that the correct quantity has been delivered.

- A **stockroom supervisor** will organise the stockroom employees and will check the deliveries for damage and quantity. They will make sure that the employees know their job roles and that the stockroom or warehouse is clean, tidy and hazard free.

- A **receptionist** is responsible for welcoming visitors and customers to the business. Their job responsibilities will include providing information and support for visitors and customers, answering phone calls and redirecting calls to relevant staff, and logging customers' calls and complaints. The receptionist is often the first employee customers will meet so it is important that they create a good image for the business.

- A **shop assistant** is responsible for providing support and information when the customer is choosing their products and then taking payment for the products. They are responsible for keeping the shop clean and tidy, and may also be responsible for stocking shelves.

Knowledge recap questions

1. How does the role of a sales-floor assistant differ from that of a sales-floor supervisor?

2. Why would someone who joined a hotel group as a receptionist look to move into customer service as a career?

Supporting retail businesses

The retail sector would not function efficiently without the support of other businesses. Businesses within the retail sector will require support and guidance when starting up, when trading and support in getting their products to the all-important customer.

The support, advice and guidance could come from a range of other businesses.

Transport and delivery companies

Studied ☐

Transport companies deliver products from the warehouse or manufacturer to retail stores. Transport and delivery companies may also be required to deliver products from the retailer to customers. The increase in online and catalogue shopping has led to an increased need for transport and delivery services.

Suppliers and manufacturers

Studied ☐

Suppliers and manufacturers are responsible for producing the products that are sold by retailers. The retail outlet will rely on the supplier and manufacturer having sufficient products available when required and supplying products that are of good quality.

Computing and financial services

Studied ☐

Companies will install computing systems and provide ongoing technical support. Financial services can provide support and guidance on banking, investments, insurance, loans and grants.

Tradespeople

Studied ☐

To keep their business running efficiently, retailers will need to rely on several different tradespeople, such as electricians and plumbers. The retail store will want tradespeople who are quality assured, reliable and professional.

Shop fitters

Studied ☐

Shop fitters will plan and fit the most appropriate fixtures, fittings and equipment for a retail store. The retail store will need to employ shop fitters who are reliable and efficient.

Marketing and advertising agencies

Studied ☐

All retail stores need to advertise their products and special promotions. They rely on marketing and advertising agencies to design appropriate materials to attract the attention of their target market.

Legal and accountancy firms

A retail store will need help with legal issues when setting up the business and when trading. It may need advice on the structure of the business, purchasing premises, employment issues, environmental issues and consumer law.

An accountant will provide support and guidance on cash flow, financing the business or any new ventures, tax and tax returns, and changes in legislation. An accountant will also produce end-of-year accounts such as the profit and loss account and the balance sheet. They will implement and conduct audits to identify any legal issues and make recommendations on how the business could run more efficiently.

Knowledge recap questions

1. Why would a convenience store employ specialist shop fitters to develop the layout of the store?

2. Accountancy firms provide a service rather than a product. How does using that service benefit a limited company?

Aims and objectives

A business' **aims** are what it wants to achieve. They might be to:

- increase market share
- improve customer service
- increase profit margin.

The **objectives** of a business are the steps that the business needs to take to achieve its identified aims.

Aims and objectives are set by the business owners and will be different for a start-up or a long-established business. The aims may also change because of internal or external factors.

The aims and objectives become the focus for what the business is working towards. The business knows what it wants to achieve and can identify the steps it will take.

For the business to remain competitive or expand it will need to assess and review the procedures it has implemented. If the business aim is to increase the profit margin, it will need to review and evaluate current procedures and identify where changes and improvements need to be made.

For a business to be successful it must set clear aims that are known by employees. To achieve these aims, the business will need to identify the steps it has to take – the objectives. The business needs to know where it is now, where it wants to be and if it has achieved its aims. The objectives need to be SMART:

- **S**pecific – clear and concise.
- **M**easureable – able to identify improvements, for example a seven per cent profit increase.
- **A**chievable – known by staff; objectives that could be accomplished.
- **R**ealistic – achievable, taking into consideration the economic environment, the market and resources available.
- **T**ime bound – the deadline by which the objective should be achieved.

Measuring performance

Key performance indicators (KPIs) are measurable targets. Depending on the size of the retail outlet it may focus on a few or several KPIs. The business will need to select the most appropriate KPIs and then use them effectively to improve the business. KPIs can be used to compare the past with the present or compare a business with its competitors.

KPIs can be introduced for:

- **sales** – growth or decline in sales
- **profit** – gross and net profit
- **sales/profit per square metre** – looking at the sales per square metre of the business premises
- **sales per employee** – the number of sales against the number of employees
- **average revenue per customer** – the average amount spent by each customer
- **service level** – customer satisfaction, including responding to customer requests
- **customer satisfaction** – analysing the feedback from customers, particularly when dealing with customer problems and complaints
- **stock holding** – stock turnover and the cost of storage
- **returns** – the volume of products that are returned and why
- **complaints** – the nature of the complaints
- **environmental performance targets** – such as air emissions and carbon footprint.

Figure 1.4 KPIs can be introduced to monitor environmental performance targets

Knowledge recap questions

1. What is the difference between an aim and an objective?

2. What are SMART objectives?

3. Why does a business set aims and objectives?

4. What are KPIs?

5. Why is profit a better measure of performance than sales?

6. Last year the average revenue per customer was £10, this year it is £8? How would you use that indicator?

7. Why are returns a good measure of performance?

8. Why would a business want to measure sales per employee?

Assessment guidance for learning aim A

2A.P1 **Describe the sub-sector, channels, format, size, ownership and location of two retail businesses operating in different sub-sectors**

✎ Learner answer

I am going to look at Greggs, a bakery that operates in the food sub-sector, and Village Lane Garage, which sells cars.

Assessor report: The command verb for 2A.P1 is describe. The learner has selected the businesses they will use and now needs to describe the sub-sector, channels, format, size, ownership and location of the businesses, including all of the relevant features.

Village Lane Garage sells and services cars. It is a local business with just one branch and has been trading for many years. Customers use the garage because it is local, it gives a friendly and prompt service and looks after its customers well. The owner has made it a private limited company because that gives him limited liability should there be any problems.

Greggs sells food products and is a PLC, so people can buy shares. It is a well-known brand and people buy there because they know the products are good. There are branches throughout the country.

Assessor report: The learner has given a good description of the garage but has not given an indication of size. They have made a good start on Greggs but not really explained enough about its ownership.

Greggs operates in the food sub-sector and is well known for its bakery products. It is a national chain and has over 1,400 branches. It is staffed locally and bakes the products on site on a daily basis, as well as making sandwiches daily. Where possible it sells local delicacies. There are branches in every major town

17

throughout the UK and it is the UK's biggest bakery chain. It aims to open a new branch each week, creating ten new jobs each time. It is a large organisation as it employs more than 250 people. It is a PLC, which means that the general public can buy shares in the business and get a share of the profits. The business itself has limited liability so the owners are not liable for any debts but the business is. By buying more shares the public invest more into Greggs so it can expand even more.

Assessor report: The learner has given a thorough answer for Greggs but needs to provide similar evidence about the garage to achieve the criterion.

Assessor report – overall

Is the evidence sufficient to satisfy the grading criterion?

The learner has produced some good work for Greggs and has started to provide some evidence for their second business, Village Lane Garage.

The learner has not yet produced sufficient evidence for 2A.P1 because they have only described part of the features of the garage. The learner could describe the size of the business and expand on its channels of retailing.

What additional evidence, if any, is required?

To achieve 2A.P1 the learner will need to provide more information on the Village Lane Garage.

2A.P2 Describe the functions of two job roles in store operations and their progression routes

✍ Learner answer

The business I have chosen to use for this part is Scent Sense, which sells perfume and cosmetics. I intend to look at the role of a retail assistant and a sales-floor supervisor.

Assessor report: The command verb for 2A.P2 is **describe**. The learner has selected the business they will use and now needs to describe the functions of two job roles in store operations and their progression routes in the business, including all of the relevant features.

Scent Sense sells a range of perfumes and cosmetics, but mainly expensive ones. The role of the sales assistant is to have knowledge of these perfumes so that they can advise the customers on what might suit them best in an unbiased way. The sales supervisor is there to make sure the assistants are doing their job, answer any queries and check that procedures are being followed.

Assessor report: The learner has identified and described the role of the sales assistant and has stated some elements of what the supervisor does. The learner will need to include more information on the functions of the supervisor and to investigate career progression routes.

Jan Forrest is the owner of Scent Sense. When new employees join the business they are given a clear job description of what the role is and the functions of the job. The sales assistant's role is to give advice to customers, provide demonstrations and ensure as many customers buy as possible. The functions are to ensure brochures are up to date; the working area is kept clean, presentable and welcoming; to ensure they have sound product knowledge and to make the customers feel valued.

Jan provides on-going training for staff about products and on how other areas of the business work. She does this so that she has staff ready trained should a vacancy occur at a higher level, or should they get the chance of promotion in another business. Jan is keen to develop 'supervisors in waiting'.

Assessor report: The learner has given an excellent answer for the sales assistant. They now need to address another role in store operations.

Assessor report – overall

Is the evidence sufficient to satisfy the grading criterion?

The learner has produced some very good work and has noted the differences between roles and functions but has not yet covered the criterion in full.

What could be improved?

The learner needs to describe the role, functions and progression routes for the sales supervisor in the store. The learner has made a good start on the second role.

Explain, using examples, the role of two businesses that support retail businesses

✍ Learner answer

I am going to look at MDS Accountancy Services and Vindy Shopfitters. I will explain what they do to support businesses in my local area. Both these businesses are specialists so they offer a good service that other businesses cannot match.

Assessor report: The command verb for 2A.P3 is **explain**; to achieve this the learner will need to set out in detail, with reasons, the role of these businesses in supporting other retail businesses.

The first paragraph is good and highlights that the learner understands the role of support businesses. They will now need to explain, with examples, how they support retail businesses.

MDS specialises in looking after the finances of small businesses. They are experts in tax law and drawing up financial statements. They charge for their services but they will save the retail businesses more than they charge, so it is worth it for the retail businesses using them. They deal with HMRC on behalf of the customer, which gives the customer peace of mind.

Assessor report: The learner has explained well what MDS does. They now need to cover the support given by Vindy Shopfitters.

Some of the local retailers know lots about their own business but not much about the financial side of their business. Some of them use MDS Accountancy Services because they are local and have a good reputation for doing a good job. This means they keep retailers on the straight and narrow with bookkeeping, balance sheets and so on, and make sure things like the right VAT is paid. The retailers have confidence in MDS and know that that part of the business is well looked after.

Vindy Shopfitters provides a good service in fitting out shops so that the places look professional. They do it better than the business could have done it themselves.

Assessor report: The learner has **explained** well what MDS does. They have **described** what Vindy does but have not explained how it supports retailers.

Is the evidence sufficient to satisfy the grading criterion?

Not quite. The learner needs to explain in much more depth how Vindy supports retailers, for example their knowledge of materials for shopfitting, suitable lighting effects, shelf layouts, and so on.

What could be improved?

The learner needs to explain how Vindy supports retailers in the way they carry out their own business using examples, as noted above.

2A.P4 Describe how two retail businesses operating in different sub-sectors make use of non-outlet retailing

✏ Learner answer

I am going to look at the Scotch Malt Whisky Society (SMWS), which sells whisky to its members by catalogue and mail order, and Amazon, which is an e-tailer. The SMWS is a small business but Amazon is very big. The SMWS operates in a niche market and in a specialised sub-sector, while Amazon sells a wide range of products, though is generally associated with books, music and DVDs.

Assessor report: The command verb for 2A.P4 is **describe**. The learner has selected the businesses they will use and now needs to describe how they make use of non-outlet retailing. The learner has made a good start and has stated in which sub-sectors each outlet operates.

Amazon makes use of non-retail selling as it has an online focus. It sells a full range of products and has a brilliant search facility, which displays results for Amazon itself and other Amazon-trusted suppliers, therefore giving people the best choice. All of this means Amazon has relatively low levels of stocks, no shop overheads and probably not as many staff as might be needed if it went retail. It has its own products, such as Kindle, which are well known. It offers great customer service as most of its products are things like books and music, which are unlikely to be returned because of 'not fitting' or similar.

Assessor report: The learner has described how Amazon operates in the non-retail sector very well. They now need to do the same for a second business.

SMWS is a private members' society so it uses mail order and online purchases only. It cannot afford to run a shop as there is no passing trade. This means it keeps overheads down and supplies what members want; when stocks run out then that is it until new stock arrives. Members know that and are happy with it. It works well for all stakeholders. They send products out via a courier service and members pay for that. It is generally cheaper than if they had to visit a store, so overall it costs less.

Amazon provides a good service as it offers next-day delivery for its online business. Everyone knows about Amazon.

Assessor report: The learner has described what SMWS does but has only made passing comments about Amazon. They need to describe how Amazon makes use of non-outlet retailing to its best advantage.

Assessor report – overall

Is the evidence sufficient to satisfy the grading criterion?

Not yet, although the learner has made some excellent points about both businesses.

What could be improved?

The learner needs to identify why this method of retailing is particularly suitable for what Amazon does, why it suits them to do this rather than have shops.

2A.P5 Describe the aims and objectives of two retail businesses operating in different sub-sectors

✍ Learner answer

> The first business I will look at is J Sainsbury PLC, which is a supermarket mainly selling grocery products. They have very clear aims and objectives, which I could find, mainly to make a profit. The second business is Butterfly Barn, which sells 'shabby chic' vintage-style soft furnishings. It is a specialised store and is operated as a partnership. Its aim is to get its brand better known.

Assessor report: The command verb for 2A.P5 is **describe**. The learner has selected the businesses they will use and now needs to describe their aims and objectives. The learner has made a good start and has stated in which sub-sectors each outlet operates as well as general ideas about their aims.

> Sainsbury's has five values that it aims to achieve, which are based on quality. This is on top of making a profit. These are long-term, ongoing aims. It uses short-term objectives such as special promotions on certain brands to highlight things like 'environmentally friendly' or 'healthy eating' to achieve its aims. **a** It measures the success of these to see if they worked.
>
> Butterfly Barn aims to make a profit and to provide a bespoke service to its customers as it will often provide made-to-measure items. They want to make internet shopping fun and personal. It does do some retail by attending craft fairs, and some other shops sell their products for them.

Assessor report: The learner has briefly described the aims of the two businesses but has only looked briefly at the objectives of one. **a** The learner has stated the aims of Sainsbury's but not described what they are. They have described what Butterfly Barn does but have not given any specific objectives.

Apart from making a profit for its shareholders, J Sainsbury PLC has five 'values', which are its aims:

- **Best for food and health** – they aim to provide great food at fair prices and to be 'best for food and health'.
- **Sourcing with integrity** – they aim to provide customers with quality products at a fair price, in a way that's better for the animals, farmers, growers and workers involved, and which minimises the impact on the environment.
- **Respect for our environment** – they aim to be the UK's greenest grocer, which is great for Sainsbury's themselves and excellent for the environment.
- **Making a positive difference to our community** – they aim to support and help communities by being a good neighbour and having stores at the heart of local developments.
- **A great place to work** – they have 150,000 workers in their stores and offices; they are the face of Sainsbury's and crucial to their business goals. They aim to look after their workforce, so being 'a great place to work' is naturally important.

(I got my information from www.j-sainsbury.co.uk/about-us/our-values) **a**

Their objectives include using things like traffic light systems on food to provide nutritional information to customers, to help drive sales. They change the merchandising, such as for their TU clothing products, to see if that helps sales, and they set targets to measure the impact. They have opened six food colleges to ensure their food is the best around by training people well.

Assessor report: The learner has described one business very well; the concept of SMART objectives is covered. The learner has used an external source and evidenced this well. **a** However, to complete the criterion another business needs to be investigated.

Assessor report – overall

Is the evidence sufficient to satisfy the grading criterion?

The learner has chosen two contrasting businesses and has described their aims very well but has not really described the objectives used to achieve those aims particularly well. They have not described any objectives for Butterfly Barn.

What could be improved?

The second business, Butterfly Barn, needs to be described fully, especially with regard to specific objectives used to achieve the set aims.

Assess two different types of ownership of selected retail businesses

✍ Learner answer

> Greggs, the bakery chain, is a PLC, which means the public can buy shares in it. Butterfly Barn is a partnership, which means the owners share everything they do and nobody else can buy into the business. These types of ownership suit the size and type of each business really well.

Assessor report: The command verb is **assess**. The learner will need to give careful consideration to all the factors that apply to their selected retail businesses and identify which are the most important or relevant to that ownership type.

The learner has set the scene by identifying which businesses they will use. The learner has given an indication that each business has specifically chosen their ownership type and has reasons for doing so.

> Butterfly Barn is a partnership. The owners have different skills and it suits them to each concentrate on what they do best. One looks after production, the other after the paperwork and running the business. They both look after design and sales.
>
> It is not a limited company, which gives them more freedom to operate how they want to. They can close the business down easily if they ever need to. Being just a two-person partnership means decision making is much quicker and communication much simpler.

Assessor report: The learner has assessed the way the business is owned and the reasons for it. However, they need to do the same for a second business.

Assessor report – overall

Is the evidence sufficient to satisfy the grading criterion?

The learner has assessed the Butterfly Barn partnership, but needs to assess the second business.

What could be improved?

To achieve 2A.M1 the learner needs to assess **two** different types of ownership. To achieve the criterion they will need to make a similar assessment for Greggs, a PLC.

2A.M2 Explain how and why two retail businesses operating in different sub-sectors use aims and objectives

✍ Learner answer

I will look at J Sainsbury PLC and Village Lane Garage as my two businesses. They both use aims and objectives, and both want to make a profit. Sainsbury's uses this aim because it has to make profit for its shareholders. The owner of Village Lane Garage wants to make money as this is his only form of income.

Whatever they do, they do it with the idea of making as much money as possible.

Assessor report: The command verb for 2A.M2 is **explain**; to achieve this the learner will need to set out in detail, with reasons, how and why two retail businesses operating in different sub-sectors use aims and objectives. This is more difficult than describe or list, so it can help to give an example to show what you mean. Start by introducing the topic then give the 'how' or 'why'.

The first paragraph is a good start and highlights that the learner understands something about aims. They will now need to **explain how and why** each uses aims and objectives in their day-to-day operations.

Village Lane Garage aims to increase its profit each year and it sets targets for each month for its sales and servicing. It advertises to bring in customers, although much of it is by word of mouth. It can then check to see how it is doing against its targets. If it has any special short-term offers on, such as a free MOT to try to get 100 extra customers over three months, it can see how well these work in bringing in extra revenue and profit. That would be a SMART objective. If it does work, it can try similar promotions. If it does not work, it can set other objectives. **a** At the end of the year it can see if it has reached its profit aim. There might be reasons why it did or did not, for example a recession, but without having specific aims and objectives it would not know if it was doing well or not. **b**

Assessor report: The learner has given a good explanation about how the garage uses aims and objectives. **a** They have also briefly explained why they have specific aims and objectives. **b** They now need to explain how a second business uses aims and objectives.

Sainsbury's uses aims and objectives to help fulfil its mission statement: 'Our mission is to be the consumer's first choice for food, delivering products of outstanding quality and great service at a competitive cost through working faster, simpler, and together.' By having this mission statement it gives a focus for any aims it has as these must relate to the mission statement. **a** They do this with their five values:

- Best for food and health.
- Sourcing with integrity.
- Respect for our environment.
- Making a positive difference to our community.
- A great place to work.

The aims mean each person in Sainsbury's has a responsibility to follow and achieve them, for example buyers of frozen foods must 'source with integrity', and the HR department needs to ensure it is 'a great place to work'. **b**

Village Lane Garage has aims and objectives to make a profit and to provide the local community with a good and friendly service for car purchase and for servicing. It supports various fund-raising appeals locally to show its support for worthy causes. This is one of its non-financial aims. It has various testimonials from charities it has helped. **c**

Assessor report: The learner has explained why Sainsbury's uses aims and objectives **a** and has given some examples of how they use aims. **b** They have also looked at Village Lane Garage's support of local charities, **c** but there is not sufficient detail about the purpose of the aim. The learner has not explained why either business uses objectives.

Assessor report – overall

Is the evidence sufficient to satisfy the grading criterion?

Not yet. The learner has made a good attempt to cover why two businesses use aims and objectives but has not really covered how they use them well.

What could be improved?

The learner has looked at two businesses and now needs to explain clearly what the aims and objectives are, then how and why they use them in the operation of their business. The objectives need to have a SMART element to them for Sainsbury's.

Evaluate how two retail businesses operating in different sub-sectors measure their performance, with reference to key performance indicators (KPIs)

✍ Learner answer

Sainsbury's measure its financial KPIs over a series of years. I found this research:

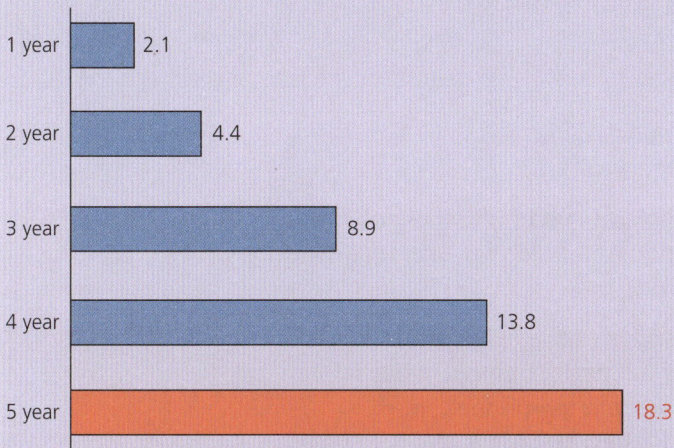

Figure 1.1 Like-for-like sales 2011/12 (%)

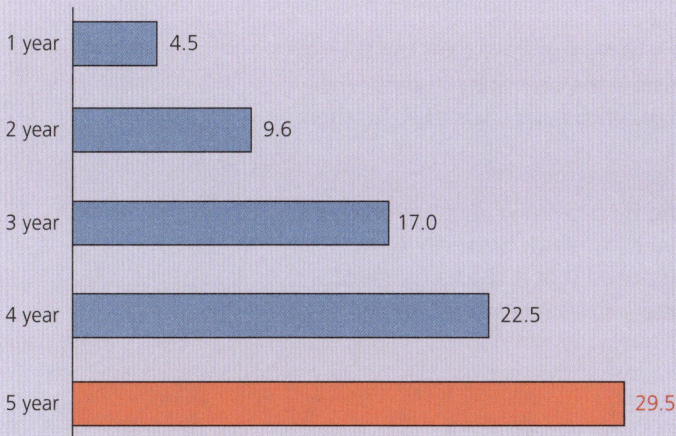

1 year	2.1
2 year	4.4
3 year	8.9
4 year	13.8
5 year	18.3

Figure 1.2 Total sales growth 2011/12 (%)

1 year	4.5
2 year	9.6
3 year	17.0
4 year	22.5
5 year	29.5

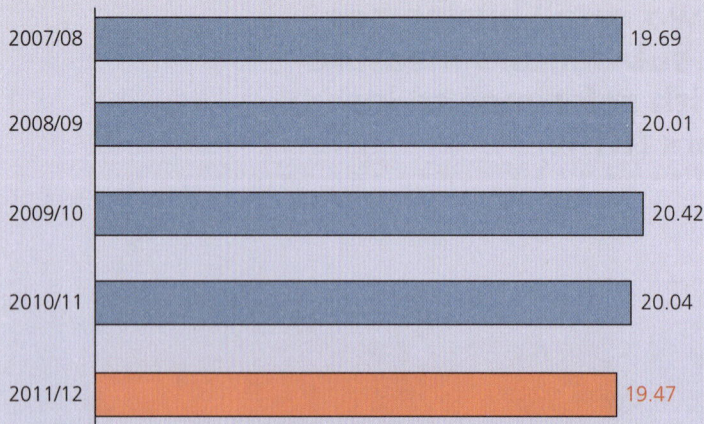

2007/08	19.69
2008/09	20.01
2009/10	20.42
2010/11	20.04
2011/12	19.47

Figure 1.3 Trading intensity per sq ft (£ per week). Reproduced by kind permission of Sainsbury's Supermarkets Ltd.

(Source: J Sainsbury plc Annual Report 2012, http://annualreport2012.j-sainsbury.co.uk)

This shows that sales have grown in each year, which is good, but the amount they got per square foot has fallen for the second year running.

Butterfly Barn uses sales, profit and average revenue per customer as financial measures of its performance. It uses returns as another measure. They keep a log of customer comments and complaints to see if they are doing the job they set out to do. This is good as it gives a range of measures, not just money measures.

Assessor report: The command verb is **evaluate**, for which the learner will need to review how two retail businesses operating in different sub-sectors measure their performance, with reference to KPIs, then bring it together to form a conclusion.

The learner has correctly set the scene by providing some excellent research on Sainsbury's use of financial KPIs. With Butterfly Barn the learner has made a good start and noted that it uses a range of measures, but they have yet to **evaluate** how the two businesses measure their performance.

Sainsbury's also uses non-financial KPIs as these link in with their aims (their five 'values'). I found some research on this and have included a sample here.

Commitments by 2020	
Best for food and health	**Progress**
Healthiest baskets	• Multiple traffic light nutritional labelling is helping customers make informed choices in-store • Product reformulation continues to reduce salt, fats and sugar in our own-brand products • Signed all the Government's Public Health Responsibility Deal food pledges, including salt and calorie reduction
Lighter alcohol	• Introduced new point-of-sale communication about responsible drinking • 14% increase in sales of lighter-alcohol wines
Sourcing with integrity	
Sustainably sourced raw materials	• Identified the top 30 raw materials in own-brand products and reviewing sourcing plans • Over 60 own-brand products made with physically certified palm oil
No 1 for fairly traded	• Strong progress towards our goal of £1 billion sales of fairly traded products by 2020 • World's largest fair-trade retailer; sales of over £288 million, up 5% on last year, accounting for 22% of all UK fair-trade sales
Best for British	• Working with over 3,000 British farmers to ensure we meet our target to double the amount of British food we sell • Largest retailer of British apples and pears for the third season; doubled the size of our British asparagus market since 2007
No 1 for animal welfare	• Leading retailer of cage-free fresh eggs and only major retailer to use cage-free eggs as ingredients in all own-brand products • Leading retailer of Freedom Food products (animals raised to strict RSPCA welfare standards) with sales of £380 million
Respect for our environment	
Packaging	• Continuous review of own-brand packaging to reduce waste, use recycled materials and/or ensure recyclability • Removed 3,000 tonnes of packaging through specific own-brand product design case studies
Operational carbon emissions	• 9.1% absolute reduction in electricity use over the past four years in our supermarkets despite a 25% increase in space • Became the largest multi-site user of photovoltaic cells in the UK, with 7MW of solar panels on 115 supermarkets

Making a positive difference to our community	
Active youth	• First ever Paralympics-only sponsor with over 2.4 million children signed up to our 1 Million Kids challenge • David Beckham became our Active Kids ambassador • Over £115 million worth of equipment donated to schools, nurseries and sports clubs since 2005 • £10 million invested in the Sainsbury's School Games competition over the next four years
Community investment	• £25.4 million contribution to over 1,000 local and national charities and community groups • £21.2 million raised by colleagues, customers and suppliers, with over 7,000 days volunteered by colleagues
A great place to work	
Commitment and engagement	• 4% increase in colleague engagement year-on-year as measured in Talkback, our annual colleague survey • 3% increase in colleagues who say they would recommend Sainsbury's as a great place to work
New jobs and skills	• Trained 18,000 colleagues in our bakery college and food colleges, with 12,200 City & Guilds certificates awarded since 2009 • Youth Can programme established to promote retail careers to young people

(Source: J Sainsbury plc Annual Report 2012, http://annualreport2012.j-sainsbury.co.uk, reproduced by kind permission of Sainsbury's Supermarkets Ltd.)

This shows specific targets that can be measured but also shows that they are not just about making a profit. This is a good point because if people know this they will view Sainsbury's as ethically good and 'green', so they are more likely to want to buy from Sainsbury's than another supermarket. It is a sort of USP for them. **a**

On the other hand, if following these KPIs makes their own-label products more expensive then some people will either not be able to afford them or decide they won't afford them, which will lose Sainsbury's sales and profit. **b**

Sainsbury's offers a brand-match service but this only applies to branded products and not own-label. They need to be confident that they can still sell enough of their own-label products at a profit to make their non-financial KPIs sustainable and achievable. **c**

Assessor report: The learner has made excellent reference to Sainsbury's use of non-financial KPIs and has evaluated them well, looking at the advantages **a** and disadvantages **b** of the KPIs used and coming to a conclusion overall. **c**

They now need to do the same for Butterfly Barn.

Sainsbury's and Butterfly Barn both use KPIs but Sainsbury's uses them more rigorously than Butterfly Barn. Sainsbury's is constantly setting targets (objectives) as a way of achieving its aims. It uses KPIs to measure rate of change as much as what they actually show, for example if revenue per customer was £30 this quarter it wouldn't mean anything, but if it had been £40 per customer last quarter then that would show a fall and it would need to look at why this happened.

Butterfly Barn uses year-on-year sales figures together with year-on-year net profit figures. This tells them if it is doing well. They also look at how many returns they get, as this will link to net profit. Also they will look at how many fairs they went to as that would impact on their sales. They are measuring efficiency all the time. It is a good way of measuring progress.

Assessor report: The learner has looked at what Butterfly Barn does but has **explained** rather than **evaluated** how they use KPIs. No conclusion has been reached about the usefulness and no negative comments, for example becoming too reliant on figures, have been addressed.

Assessor report – overall

Is the evidence sufficient to satisfy the grading criterion?

The learner has evaluated the use of a wide range of KPIs for one business only (Sainsbury's).

What could be improved?

The learner needs to evaluate a range of KPIs for Butterfly Barn, using a similar approach to that used for Sainsbury's.

Learning aim B
Investigate the relationship between retail business and the external environment

Learning aim B looks at the impact the external environment can have on a retail business. It examines how developments in the retail sector can have a positive impact on a local community. It also focuses on the issues for a retail business that wants to move into international markets.

Assessment criteria

2B.P6	Explain, using examples, two issues of concern and two benefits that can arise from retail developments in the UK.
2B.P7	Explain, using examples, three issues facing UK retail businesses when they decide to operate in another country.
2B.M3	Assess the benefits for the local community of a retail development in the UK.
2B.D2	Evaluate the impact of a retail development in the UK on the local community.

Retail business in the UK

UK retail businesses and the external environment: issues

Studied ☐

The retail business is constantly changing, with retailers moving away from traditional high street locations and some entirely focusing on internet sales. A retail business is not only affected by developments and changes in the sector but also by the impact of environmental changes.

Environmental issues

Today everyone is more aware of environmental issues and customers will look to purchase from a retail business that is taking responsible steps to preserve the environment.

- The increase in **road traffic** affects the environment but customers rely on transport companies to deliver purchases from television shopping channels and websites. A retail business could ensure that they use a fuel-efficient distribution network.
- Media discussion concerning **carbon footprints** is making businesses look at introducing more efficient ways to save energy and water; this also helps to reduce their overheads.

- Most retail products come in **packaging** but businesses could keep packaging to a minimum and use recyclable materials.
- Customers are more aware of **food miles** (how far and by what means food has travelled before reaching the retail outlet). A business should find the most environmentally friendly way to transport food.
- **Green site development** of land which could be used for agriculture and farming, but which is used for homes, retail developments and offices. It reduces the amount of land available for farming, which could drive up food prices. The development work involves a lot of disruption, for example building new roads, which contributes to noise and air pollution in the area. Any building work, and the transport involved, creates more carbon dioxide, which adds to global warming.

Figure 2.1 Businesses should be aware of their food miles

Ethical issues

Customers' buying habits are often influenced by information in the media. In the past few years there has been an increase in the number of customers who are ethically conscious – they prefer to buy fair-trade products, which support the poorest and weakest producers, and will not purchase products produced by child labour or that are tested on animals. Customers will buy products from a business that has ethical policies and trades with other businesses who have similar procedures.

Consumers today are more aware of how foods are grown and produced; they may be reluctant to purchase genetically modified foods but will pay a little extra for organic foods.

Customers are also increasingly aware of the importance of a healthier lifestyle, and most retail stores now sell products that clearly display the levels of fat, salt, sugar and calories for consumers. The increase in women returning to full-time work and extended and flexible working hours saw an increase in the purchase of convenience, processed foods, but with the escalation in health problems and more media coverage on the benefits of a healthier lifestyle, more customers today may choose fresh foods over processed foods.

Community concerns

The changes and developments in the retail sector have seen many stores move away from the high street to the outskirts of town. These out-of-town developments usually include a supermarket, which sells a wide variety and range of products, is open longer hours and provides free parking. Customers will look at the most convenient way to purchase products and, if everything is provided in the supermarket, they will not need to visit the town centre. The introduction of non-food items in supermarkets has impacted on retail outlets that sell clothes, household items, electrical items and DVDs. Small retail stores such as butchers or fruit shops located in town centres struggle to compete with supermarket prices. The increase in out-of-town developments and their cheaper prices have seen shops in town centres and smaller retail stores close their doors.

Customers need transport to get to any retail store. Any out-of-town supermarket or retail outlet will create an increase in traffic and this often requires changes to road layouts, with additional traffic lights and pedestrian walkways or crossings being created. Any changes to the road structure will incur costs for the local council, which then may impact on the council tax paid by local residents.

Political issues

The supermarkets have impacted on both town-centre shops and small independent retailers, but customers do benefit from competition between the large supermarkets such as Tesco, Asda, Morrisons and Sainsbury's. The Competition Commission ensures that there is healthy competition between these companies, which often leads to lower prices and a better service for customers. There have been several disputes over supermarkets dominating the retail sector, but an inquiry by the Competition Commission highlighted that the supermarkets were providing a good deal for consumers.

There have been several protests against plans to build out-of-town retail developments, with local MPs and residents raising concerns about the impact on the environment, the town centre and small retail outlets. Some campaigns have been successful and the plans for new developments have been declined.

Retail stores need to advertise but there are restrictions on advertising, including what can be advertised on TV before the 9 p.m. watershed. Retail outlets have been told to amend their advertising campaigns following complaints by other retailers and customers when advertising is misleading.

Benefits of retail developments to communities and customers

`Studied ☐`

The changes and developments in the retail sector have brought many benefits to communities and customers.

Economic benefits

The introduction of any retail development will have a positive impact on the community. The new business is likely to provide job opportunities. The retail development may also improve the local area, by developing ground that has become overgrown and an eyesore. Any improvement in the area may attract people to move there and other stores to open. The outcome of more people moving into the area will be more customers and increased sales.

Retail stores and supermarkets are well known for sponsoring events, such as sports events (Sainsbury's, for example, sponsored the London 2012 Paralympics). Small local retailers often sponsor or donate money or prizes for local charity or voluntary events (for example charity bike rides). In most town centres there are shops that collect and sell products for charities.

Social benefits

Most large retail outlets, supermarkets and retail parks have cafes or restaurants where customers can meet with family and friends or take a welcome rest with colleagues during lunch breaks. Retail outlets and retail parks are designed to encourage customers to spend time there by providing seating, staging events or providing play areas for children.

Customer benefits

Retail developments are designed to provide easy access for all customers and often have free parking, with designated parking spaces for parents with young children and customers with disabilities. Most stores provide trolleys with seats for children and some provide trolleys that can be attached to wheelchairs. The larger retail outlets have lifts and moving walkways which provide easy access between the different levels. The majority of large retail outlets and supermarkets also have petrol stations where the petrol is often cheaper than at local garages.

Knowledge recap questions

1. Businesses are encouraged to reduce the carbon footprint involved in their products by reducing air miles used. What benefits will this bring the business?

2. How could a business that specialises in packaging materials help the environment while not losing any sales?

3. Why is it better to use a brownfield site for a new retail park rather than a greenfield site?

4. How will retailers benefit from selling organic vegetables rather than processed ones?

5. A retail park with several leading supermarkets and chain stores is built on land near a small village. State the positive and negative effects that this will have on the village.

Doing business with the rest of the world

All retail businesses want to be successful and, once they have become established in the UK, they may consider moving into international markets. When the business decides the time is right to trade in international markets, there are several issues that need to be considered.

- **Language** – there may be language barriers; not everyone understands or speaks fluent English.
- **Currency** – the business will need to be aware of current exchange rates.

Figure 2.2 Exchange rates are an important factor to consider when trading in international markets

- **Customs** – to be successful it is important to research the intended international market to develop a better understanding of their potential customers' needs and, of course, the competition. Research will help the business know and understand the different customs so that they do not offend or upset customers.
- **Styles, tastes and lifestyles** – the retailer may need to adapt the products or packaging to meet the different tastes, styles and lifestyles of their potential customers.
- **Cultural considerations** – the business will need to consider whether the products are appropriate or if there will be barriers to customers purchasing the products. For example, some religions do not allow certain meats to be eaten; vegetarians need to be assured that no meat-related products, for example gelatine, have been used in processed food; some people will only buy free-range eggs and/or products made with free-range eggs.

- **Self-entry** – the retail business could set up overseas with a small office staffed by employees from the UK or employ local people to run the store. The business would need to know the local laws, including employment and tax.
- **Acquisition** – the retail business could decide that the best way to expand is by making an acquisition of another business. This is when the business purchases another business and ends up running and controlling it. It could be costly but an advantage may be that the business already has established links with customers and suppliers.
- **Franchising** – the retail business will be selling products under the brand and trademark of the franchisor.
- **Joint ventures** – the retail business could consider a joint venture with a business located abroad. The benefits would be the knowledge that business would have of local tastes, customs and styles.
- **Location issues** – the retail business will need to decide if they are going to trade solely on the internet or if they are going to open a store abroad. In the global marketplace, the internet is an uncomplicated way to export goods internationally whereas it will take time and resources to open an overseas store. However, the store will provide the opportunity to get to know the country and the customers whereas the internet may be a little impersonal.
- **Economic and legislative environments** – legislation varies from country to country and products or packaging may have to be amended to comply with local laws and regulations. The business will need to be aware of the required standards for products and any export legislation. The business would need to understand the economic climate of the country they want to export to. The retail business may face problems if there is an unstable economic environment or any political conflict.

Knowledge recap questions

1. Why would a business that is doing well in the UK want to enter into a joint venture with a similar business overseas rather than just set up there?

2. What is meant by the term self-entry?

3. Why would a business selling pork pies need to be careful when looking to expand its business overseas?

4. If the pound is strong in value compared with another currency, why is it not a good idea for a business to start selling its goods abroad?

Assessment guidance for learning aim B

(2B.P6) **Explain, using examples, two issues of concern and two benefits that can arise from retail developments in the UK**

✍ Learner answer

> Two concerns that arise from retail developments are the loss of jobs in local shops and increased traffic in areas where it had been quiet.
>
> Two benefits are that new jobs will be created and there will be better transport links.

Assessor report: The command verb for 2B.P6 is explain; to achieve this the learner needs to set out in detail, with examples, two issues of concern and two benefits that arise from retail developments. This is more difficult than describe or list, so it can help to give an example to show what you mean. Start by introducing the topic then give the 'how' or 'why'.

The learner has listed two concerns and two benefits but has not yet explained them. They have used the same issues as both a benefit and a concern. To achieve the criterion, the learner needs to use more than 'reverse arguments'.

> The redevelopment of our town centre caused some concerns but it brought some benefits as well. Many people were divided on their view.
>
> People thought that new supermarkets selling more fashionable clothes and at better prices would be a good thing as it would bring more choice, **a** but others worried that some of these products were not ethically produced so we shouldn't support them. **b**
>
> Most people thought that the new development would bring more employment, for example for builders, **a** but some people thought the developers would use their own labour from out of the area so we wouldn't benefit **b** and there would be a lot of disruption and noise while it was all going on. **b**
>
> Some people liked the idea of more shops and more competition as it meant more choice, **a** but some local shops thought it would put them out of business. **b**

The developers said they would encourage food franchises such as McDonald's to set up in town, but people said that would only cause more litter. **b** Other people liked the idea because it would mean they wouldn't have to travel as far to get their favourite food. **a**

Assessor report: The learner has made a good start by identifying concerns **b** and benefits. **a** The work is descriptive of the arguments surrounding the development but has not yet focused on explaining why the concerns and benefits exist, for example that the new McDonald's might be a **benefit** by bringing more part-time employment and boosting the local economy; a **concern** was that some shops would lose out to the big supermarkets because they couldn't compete on range or prices and they might not have enough money to be able to fight them with the Competition Commission.

When a new retail development is suggested people get concerned about the impact on local retailers not being able to compete with some of the bigger multiples, especially on price. This is mainly the retailers themselves, but many local people want to shop in local shops where they can buy in small amounts; if too many people start going to the new shops then the local retailer will close down, so some locals would lose out. This is a concern as some people might not be able to travel to the new development or it might cost more than they would save on the food. **a**

People like buying locally because products, for example vegetables and meat, are often sourced locally so they know it has been produced ethically and possibly organically as well. People like the idea of the community working together. A concern with a new retail development is that they couldn't be as certain about the source of the food. People are much more aware of ethical issues and healthy eating these days, so this is an important concern. **a**

Assessor report: The learner has explained two concerns very well and given good examples to back up their explanations. **a** To achieve the criterion the learner now needs to look at benefits as well.

Assessor report – overall

Is the evidence sufficient to satisfy the grading criterion?

Correct issues have been identified across a suitable range and the learner has made some very good points about concerns arising from retail developments. The work is well structured and needs only some development to achieve the criterion.

What could be improved?

To achieve 2B.P6 the learner needs to build on the work provided by explaining two benefits, with examples, of the retail development.

Explain, using examples, three issues facing UK retail businesses when they decide to operate in another country

✍ Learner answer

> It is always difficult for a business to operate in another country. The sort of issues they will face include whether to set up themselves overseas or go into a joint venture with an existing business, different laws and whether it is cost-effective to transport the goods abroad.

Assessor report: The command verb for 2B.P7 is **explain**; to achieve this the learner will need to set out in detail, with examples, the issues facing UK retail businesses when they decide to operate in another country. This is more difficult than describe or list, so it can help to give an example to show what you mean. Start by introducing the topic then give the 'how' or 'why'.

The learner has made a good start and has identified three issues but has not yet explained these issues.

> Businesses have to be very careful when they decide they want to operate outside the UK as it may require a complete change in the way they go about things. They may decide to try and set up their franchise in another country, but the laws about things like health and safety and advertising might be different.
>
> A business might decide to set up a joint venture with a local business overseas, which might be a better idea than setting up on their own.
>
> Rather than pay for transport and rent, a business might decide to launch a website to make its products more widely known and available.

Assessor report: The learner has **identified** three different issues that a business would face. There is some description on them but no real explanation or examples given.

One issue a business has to decide on is whether to set up themselves overseas or go into a joint venture with an existing business. A sports retailer might find it easier to work with an existing retailer abroad as the overseas retailer may have a good local reputation, so people will trust them better than a new retailer. The existing retailer will have a better knowledge of what sells locally, for example football shirts might sell well in the UK but may not be as popular as another product abroad. **a** The local retailer will know better about what sort of advertising is allowed and what is not suitable. That will save the UK retailer money. **b** If a retailer was thinking of going down the self-entry route abroad, they might face a lot of opposition locally if they only brought in UK staff to run the business. This might stop the business getting going at all.

Assessor report: The learner has explained one issue very well (whether to set up themselves or go into a joint venture) and has provided good examples. **a** A second issue has been identified and a description of the problem has been given (local advertising laws) **b** but needs to be explained in more detail. The learner also needs to explain a third issue.

Assessor report – overall

Is the evidence sufficient to satisfy the grading criterion?

The learner has stated some very relevant issues facing UK retailers thinking of operating in another country but needs to develop the answers in places and ensure that three issues are fully addressed.

What could be improved?

To achieve 2B.P7 the learner needs to make sure they explain three issues (at the moment they have only covered one in detail). They could add examples to do with lifestyle (for example working hours), adapting the products (for example transporting perishable goods), or changes to production methods.

2B.M3 Assess the benefits for the local community of a retail development in the UK

✍ Learner answer

> MM Retail Park has been developed on a site in a quiet and previously unspoilt area of the UK. It has brought many benefits to the local community, including developing unused land, attracting lots of high-street shops and restaurants, and building a play park.

Assessor report: The command verb for 2B.M3 is **assess**. The learner will need to give careful consideration to all the factors that benefit the local community as a result of a retail development in the UK and identify which are the most important or relevant.

The learner has introduced the retail development they will use in their answer, and has listed some of the benefits, but now needs to **assess** these benefits for the local community.

> The retail park was built outside our town where some old factories used to be. The land was a waste and a bit ugly. It is close to a dual carriageway so getting to it is quite easy. The developers were really good; they talked to local people about what sort of shops and amenities they wanted, and generally got people on-board with it all. It meant they had no opposition.
>
> The locals were happy because the only new roads that were needed were on the park itself. By bringing in big companies like Asda and Boots the local people are able to shop more cheaply and they can buy their petrol more cheaply as well. **a**
>
> Overall, it has been a good thing.

Assessor report: The learner has **described** the new development quite well and given some reasons why it has benefited the local community (economic benefits such as cheaper petrol) but has not yet **assessed** the benefits or made reference to which developments are the most important.

The retail park is midway between two bigger towns. They have built some roads to make access easier but this has not taken up much land. DPO Developments built the retail park and it has worked so well that people just know it now as 'DP'.

They have brought in all the major brand shops but have done much more than that. Most of the big stores have in-store cafes, which has been very helpful to the community because people can shop a bit, have a coffee, do some more shopping, sit and chat with friends then go off again. Some stores have provided lockers where you can leave your trolley then go somewhere else and come back for it later. People like that as it means they don't have to lug loads of shopping round with them. What has happened is that people use DP to meet up as well as shop, and this has really developed the community spirit. You hear people greeting other 'regulars' whom they've got to recognise just by seeing them there. Already people are working with DP to put on Christmas projects together. **b**

Many food outlets and restaurants have been encouraged to set up there and the developers have worked closely with local people to 'add value' to the development. They have done this by providing things such as play areas for different age groups. This has been important as children can get bored with shopping and this gives them a release. It has worked well as it encourages the children to play together and the parents, mostly mums, get a chance to chat. **b**

Because the parking is free, people use DP regularly.

Assessor report: The learner has made a very good assessment of the social benefits of the new development, but now needs to look at another benefit.

Assessor report – overall

Is the evidence sufficient to satisfy the grading criterion?

The learner has made a good assessment of the social benefits of the development. **b** The learner has also laid a good foundation for assessing the economic benefits, but has stopped at the description level. **a**

What could be improved?

To achieve criterion 2B.M3 the learner needs to assess a second benefit provided by DPO Developments. They could develop their discussion of the economic benefits **b** into an assessment.

2B.D2 Evaluate the impact of a retail development in the UK on the local community

✍ Learner answer

Since DPO Developments built the retail park known as 'DP', there is more road noise due to the extra traffic. This is a bad thing. However, there are more jobs available, which is good.

Assessor report: The command verb for 2B.D2 is **evaluate**; the learner will need to review the information relating to the impact of a retail development in the UK on the local community, looking at the advantages and disadvantages and then bringing it together to form a conclusion. The learner needs to give evidence for each point of view or statement.

The learner has acknowledged that for an evaluation both negatives and positives need to be addressed. The learner has made a good start by listing one of each.

When DP was built people were very worried about increased traffic and noise. They did build some new roads but local people benefited as they could use them to get to other parts of the area. There was some extra noise but it depended where you lived. You got used to it and now I don't notice it at all. **a**

People were needed to build the extra roads which brought some much-needed employment. This meant people had more money to spend, so the local economy did well. Overall, this proved to be a good thing.

Most people like to visit DP for 'retail therapy'. People usually spend more than they intend to, but that helps the local retailers that have an outlet there.

Assessor report: The learner has provided a very good evaluation of the impact of an environmental issue (traffic), giving a balanced argument and making a justified judgement. **a** They now need to look at other issues.

The announcement that DPO Developments were going to build a new retail park caused a lot of interest.

Some people got jobs with the building work but a few have lost jobs in the village because some trade has dried up. A lot of those who lost jobs were only part-time so it didn't hit them really hard. Some of them found work on the new park.

There was a lot of talk from the 'green' people about the carbon footprint that all the extra traffic would bring, and that a lot of the food in the supermarkets would be high in 'food miles'. Most people agreed when asked but only buy the organic stuff when it suits them. There is a shop that bases its products' advertising on being not tested on animals. Everyone is pleased they are there. People are very ethical and feel it is the right thing to do. Nobody was against this and people did like having that store nearby.

Some local shops lost out and people did feel sorry for them. A lot of the older residents relied on those local shops. They don't have, or want, the internet so can't use the home delivery service shops at DP offer. A few people have offered to get their shopping - a nice gesture that has brought out good feelings towards each other, but the older residents still feel robbed a bit.

Overall, though, there is more choice, more competition, better prices and people enjoy going to DP. There have been some bad things from DP being built but it has brought more benefits than drawbacks.

Assessor report: The learner has made a very good evaluation of three of the issues relating to retail business and the external environment. The learner has not fully evaluated the range of benefits that emerge for this retail development.

Assessor report – overall

Is the evidence sufficient to satisfy the grading criterion?

The learner has made some very valid evaluative comments about retail developments and has grasped the concept of evaluation well. However, there is a lack of balance between issues arising from retail developments and the benefits that this brings to the local community.

What could be improved?

To achieve 2B.D2 the learner needs to address the political issues from retail developments such as DP and to evaluate the benefits that they bring to the local community.

Sample assignment brief for learning aim A

PROGRAMME NAME:	BTEC Level 2 First Award in Business
ASSESSOR:	
DATE ISSUED:	SUBMISSION DATE:
INTERIM REVIEW:	

This assignment will assess the following learning aim and grading criteria:

A Explore the structure and organisation of retail business

2A.P1 Describe the sub-sector, channels, format, size, ownership and location of two retail businesses operating in different sub-sectors.

2A.P2 Describe the functions of two job roles in store operations and their progression routes.

2A.P3 Explain, using examples, the role of two businesses that support retail businesses.

2A.P4 Describe how two retail businesses operating in different sub-sectors make use of non-outlet retailing.

2A.P5 Describe the aims and objectives of two retail businesses operating in different sub-sectors.

2A.M1 Assess two different types of ownership of selected retail businesses.

2A.M2 Explain how and why two retail businesses operating in different sub-sectors use aims and objectives.

2A.D1 Evaluate how two retail businesses operating in different sub-sectors measure their performance, with reference to key performance indicators (KPIs).

Scenario

Carol-Ann Riddin is a business editor for a TV company. She is looking for material for a new show called *Retail Detail*, where she covers retail-related topics and where people can ring in for advice. She has asked you to do some research which you'll have the chance to present live on the programme.

Carol-Ann is very clear about what she wants and has set a series of tasks to cover this material. She is keen that researchers use local examples where possible.

Task 1

You have to find **two** businesses from different sub-sectors and with different types of ownership. For each one produce a slideshow describing:

- what the sub-sector is
- what the business does
- the ownership type
- how big the business is
- where it is located
- how it advertises and sells its products
- the aims and objectives of each business, noting things that are the same and things that are different
- an explanation of how and why these two businesses use these aims and objectives in the way they manage the progress of the business.

Task 2

These businesses need staff. Carol-Ann wants you to produce leaflets that describe:

- a job role in the first business
- a different job role in the second business
- how you could make progress and get promotion in each of them.

(There should be separate leaflets for the job role and for the promotion routes.)

Task 3

Carol-Ann wants a written report that she can use to advise callers on what is out there to support them.

Select **two** businesses that provide different types of support. For the businesses you have used in Task 1, you will need to explain:

- who they are
- where they are based
- what they do
- why each business would use them rather than do that job themselves.

The support services could be:

- transport and delivery companies
- suppliers and manufacturers
- financial services
- tradespeople, such as electricians or maintenance engineers
- shop fitters
- marketing and advertising agencies
- legal advisers
- accountancy firms.

Task 4

Carol-Ann has had a call from a company called Nobler Lyrics that sells sheet music, CDs and vinyl LPs. It does not have a shop because it thinks the overheads are too high. It wants some advice about other ways to sell its products. Carol-Ann agrees to help.

Create an information booklet that describes:
1. What non-outlet retailing is.
2. How **two** businesses from different sub-sectors use non-outlet retailing, for example:

- mail order
- e-tailing
- catalogues
- telephone selling
- vending machines
- TV shopping programmes.

3. The benefits of using these channels to sell their products.

Task 5

Diane has set up a little business called Winter Draws On, which makes handmade Christmas cards, calendars and decorations. She has more enquiries than she expected and is looking to expand. She has rung to ask advice about the best type of ownership for her.

Carol-Ann thinks it would be a good idea to have a live debate about this on the show. She has asked you to look at the businesses you presented in Task 1 and to prepare scripts for two presenters.
Each script must assess a different type of ownership, looking at:

- the factors that led the business to choose that form of ownership
- the benefits that ownership type has brought the business.

In response to your request Carol-Ann has agreed you can use other businesses but they *must* be of different ownership types.

Task 6

Carol-Ann is very impressed with your work and with the viewing figures. Viewing figures are one major method that TV companies use to measure their performance. Her boss calls it a KPI (key performance indicator).

She is keen to find out about KPIs in the retail world and how retail businesses use them to measure performance. She thinks this would make good viewing.
She suggests:

- Is there one standard measure?
- Do they measure against targets?
- Or against each other?
- What is judged as success?
- Is it measured year-on-year?

Keen to continue your success, you agree to evaluate how two retail businesses from different sub-sectors measure their performance using KPIs.

You give Carol-Ann the following as examples of KPIs, but tell her that the two businesses you investigate may use others:

- sales
- profit
- sales/profit per square metre
- sales per employee
- average revenue per customer
- service level
- customer satisfaction
- stock holding
- returns
- complaints
- environmental performance targets.

In response to your request Carol-Ann has agreed you can use the businesses you used earlier or other businesses, but they *must* be from different sub-sectors.

Sample assignment brief for learning aim B

PROGRAMME NAME:	BTEC Level 2 First Award in Business
ASSESSOR:	
DATE ISSUED:	SUBMISSION DATE:
INTERIM REVIEW:	

This assignment will assess the following learning aim and grading criteria:

B Investigate the relationship between retail business and the external environment.

2B.P6 Explain, using examples, two issues of concern and two benefits that can arise from retail developments in the UK.

2B.P7 Explain, using examples, three issues facing UK retail businesses when they decide to operate in another country.

2B.M3 Assess the benefits for the local community of a retail development in the UK.

2B.D2 Evaluate the impact of a retail development in the UK on the local community.

Scenario

Continuing your work for *Retail Detail*, Carol-Ann has given you the task of being a roving reporter looking at issues that affect local communities when there is a development in their retail environment.

Gyrwy is a town in the north of England where unemployment is rising. The local town centre is becoming run down and many small local businesses are closing down.

Local and national governments are keen to redevelop the area by selling off the shopping centre and creating a retail park. Many of the big multiples such as Tesco, Boots and Currys have said they would put a store in the retail park.

Task 1

Carol-Ann has asked you to write a report that:

1. Explains the issues of concern that local people in the area might have about this proposed development. These could be:

   - environmental
   - ethical
   - community
   - political.

2. Explains the benefits to the local community that may arise from the development. These could be:

   - economic
   - social
   - customer-based.

For the report to have appeal you need to give **specific examples**.

Task 2

In order to bring the report to a conclusion, Carol-Ann wants you to assess the benefits of the proposed development on the local community. She suggests you look at things such as:

- job opportunities
- new transport systems
- improved recreational facilities.

Task 3

Following the show being on TV there is even more local reaction, as not everyone believes they will benefit from the proposed development.

The local council wants more information. Because of your in-depth research they have asked you to evaluate the impact of the development on the local community.

Produce a leaflet with the valid points included. This will help them make a final decision about whether to go ahead.

Task 4

Carol-Ann is delighted that the KPI of viewing figures continues to rise. She is approached by a large bakery business that currently sells the usual bakery products but also local delicacies such as:

- Ham and pease pudding stotties
- Saveloy dips
- Lardie cakes
- Cornish pasties.

The bakery is thinking of expanding overseas and wants to know what factors it would need to consider if it decided to operate in another country. Carol-Ann has given this job to you.

Use your research to produce some guidance for them to consider before beginning to operate in another country. Prepare a booklet, which could be used by other retailers as well, that explains three issues facing UK retailers when they decide to operate in other countries, using examples from other businesses. These could include:

- local customs
- lifestyles
- franchising
- joint ventures
- legislation
- exchange rate concerns
- culture.

Knowledge recap answers: learning aim A

The nature of retailing and retail sub-sectors

1. The wholesaler will buy in bulk, so the manufacturer will only make one delivery and so cut costs. They will probably be able to sell all their stock that way rather than have some left over.
2. The peas start off with the farmer who picks them. They are then transported to a factory to freeze and pack them. Then they are taken by refrigerated lorries to the depots of the retailer or wholesaler. The retailer will put them on sale straightaway in the freezer section; the wholesaler will store them in a freezer until a smaller retailer buys them for resale.
3. Any retailer selling similar products irrespective of the size of the retailer, for example the DIY sub-sector could include anything from a village shop selling paint and so on, through to B&Q with its chain of outlets.
4. Footwear, electrical, automotive, grocery, music, homewares, wine.

Retail business ownership

1. The general public can buy shares in a public limited company; they cannot do so with a private limited company, where only invited investors can buy shares.
2. The franchisor sells the franchise, for example Subway; the franchisee buys the franchise, i.e. the local manager.
3. They would have separate skills that could complement each other, for example one could do the cutting and one could do the paperwork. It would be easier for each one to take a holiday. They could share ideas on how to progress.

Retail outlets

1. **a.** Fewer than nine people.
   b. Ten to 249 people.
   c. More than 250 people.
2. A department store has separate departments selling a range of franchised brands, for example ladies hats; each mini-franchise is run individually. A chain store such as M&S has departments but only sells its own brand and is run totally by the store itself.
3. Customers might work late and not want to make another journey to find a large super-market, so they will just use the 'shop on the corner'. It might not be efficient in terms of fuel to travel to a supermarket if they only need one item. Many customers like to support their local store if they can.

Non-outlet retailing

1. Because they can demonstrate the products in a dynamic way and show exactly what it can do. It also allows for more persuasive advertising by getting recommendations on air. Customers can see the benefits the product would bring them.
2. One advantage is that there would be a greater range from which to choose. Another is that there will be a greater price range from which to choose.
   One disadvantage is that it would not be possible to try the dress on before you buy it. Another might be that there could be a problem if you wanted to return the dress. Another would be that it could be difficult to get it altered.
3. Customers get a catalogue and place an order by phone or online. A courier delivers the goods. If the customer does not want the goods the courier will return to collect them and return them to the supplier. Most mail-order companies offer credit terms to allow customers to pay for the goods in instalments.

Location

1. The premises are usually larger, so more stock can be held and displayed. Parking is better and usually free, so customers will be happy to browse. Customers have to make a trip to a retail park, so they go with the intention to purchase.
2. If a customer has gone out with the intention of buying a car, it cuts down on the travelling for the customer and makes comparisons quicker and easier. The customer can return to a showroom quickly for more information. Overall, the customer is more likely to buy if all the information they need is available in one place.
3. **a.** On the high street, so more convenient for customers; higher overheads than secondary locations.
   b. Less competition for businesses sited there; usually has free parking for customers.

Jobs in retail business

1. The sales-floor assistant deals directly with the customer and is responsible only for that specific job. The sales-floor supervisor might deal with customers but their main task is to ensure that the sales assistants are doing their job properly.

2. Because they will have had training on dealing with customers face-to-face and will have had the opportunity to show they can provide a good service in the receptionist environment. If they are good at that and enjoy it, they may want to develop that skill in other areas of customer service in the hotel, for example sales.

Supporting retail businesses

1. Because they are specialists in what they do. They will be more efficient than the store owner at doing this. They have more experience and a wider range of ideas from similar jobs they have done before. They will do a better job overall.

2. They are experts on accounting procedures that a limited company must follow. They will keep the finances of the limited company correct and legal. Although the accountancy firm will charge a fee, it is likely that the limited company will save more money than they pay out due to the expertise of the accountants. By using an accountancy firm, the limited company can focus more on its own business.

Aims and objectives, and measuring performance

1. An aim is a long-term goal of what the business wants to achieve. An objective is a short-term strategy on how to make progress towards that aim. A business will use a series of objectives to achieve its overall aim.

2. Objectives towards the business' aim that are:
   - **S**pecific – clear and concise.
   - **M**easureable – able to identify improvements, for example a seven per cent profit increase.
   - **A**chievable – known by staff; objectives that could be accomplished.
   - **R**ealistic – achievable, taking into consideration the economic environment, the market and resources available.
   - **T**ime bound – the deadline by which the objective should be achieved.

3. So that it can set targets for the set objectives that can be measured to see if its progress is in line with its overall aim. If not, the business can review what it is doing and set new objectives or aims.

4. Key performance indicators.

5. Because it's profit that really counts. You can have high sales but not a lot of profit if you've discounted the price on the goods.

6. It might show you that customers were spending less when they came into your shop. Or it might show there is a recession on if you were selling the same amount but you had to reduce the prices to sell the stock. Or you might have more competition, so customers are going elsewhere.

7. Because it tells you whether you are selling the right products with the right quality and price. If you get a lot of returns then maybe the sales staff sold customers the wrong product or maybe the quality is not as good as it was, or a competitor was offering a better deal.

8. This would be a measure of how well each one was doing compared with each other or against a target. It would show who was working hardest for the business. You would have to measure returns as well to make sure they weren't just making any old sale just to get their own figures up.

Knowledge recap answers: learning aim B

Retail business in the UK

1. They will reduce the costs of the raw material or manufactured products as less fuel has to be paid for by the producer. Many customers like to buy more 'ethical' goods so they will be attracted by this. It is a good selling/advertising point, so they will get more sales.
2. They could start using material that are recyclable and are produced from renewable resources. Although this might seem to reduce sales initially, they would get a good reputation that people would want to be associated with, so sales would go up.
3. Because the land has already been used by industry so it is not suitable for growing food and keeping animals on. This would help keep the countryside. There may be some existing buildings that could be reused rather than building new ones.
4. They would not have to pay for the processing costs, so the vegetables might be cheaper. They might be able to get them locally, so that would save money. Customers expect to pay more for organic vegetables as they feel they are better and want to do their bit to help the environment, so the business could increase its profits that way.
5. Positive:
   - More employment directly and in support sectors, for example cleaning, building.
   - More money being spent in the local economy.
   - Greater choice for the villagers.
   - Better infrastructure.

   Negative:
   - May lose village stores.
   - Some unemployment.
   - Noise and air pollution.
   - Houses may lose value.

Doing business with the rest of the world

1. The other business would have much greater knowledge of local laws, customs, expectations, the economy and so on. They will already have a customer base and will probably have a good reputation that they can trade on, all of which the UK business does not yet have.
2. A UK business setting up overseas but owned, staffed and run by UK personnel.
3. Because the product might not be acceptable in certain areas and they would need to be aware of local customs, beliefs, trading standards, competition and laws.
4. If the pound is strong then UK goods will be more expensive overseas, so people might be able to buy a similar product locally for less, or they may be able to buy a similar product from a country with a weaker currency, again for less. The UK business could easily end up with too much stock overseas and be forced to sell it at a loss.

R.88173